**AUTHENTIC TRANSCRIPTIONS
WITH NOTES AND TABLATURE**

**Transcribed by
DANNY BEGELMAN**

BLACK SABBATH
PARANOID

ISBN 978-0-7935-6729-4

HAL•LEONARD®
CORPORATION
7777 W. BLUEMOUND RD. P.O. BOX 13819 MILWAUKEE, WI 53213

Visit Hal Leonard Online at
www.halleonard.com

BLACK SABBATH
PARANOID

BLACK SABBATH
PARANOID

War Pigs

Words and Music by Frank Iommi, John Osbourne, William Ward and Terence Butler

Bridge

Gtr. 2: w/ Rhy. Fig. 2, 1st time

N.C.(E5)

1. Pol - i - ti - cian's hide them - selves a - way, ___
2. Time will tell ___ on their ___ pow - er ___ minds, ___

Gtr. 1   Gtrs. 1 & 2

P.M.   P.M.   1/2   P.M.   P.M.   1/2

they on - ly start - ed the ___ war. ___
mak - ing war ___ Just for fun. ___

Riff A   End Riff A

P.M.   P.M.   1/2   P.M.   P.M.   1/2

Gtrs. 1 & 2: w/ Riff A, 2 times

Why should they ___ go out to ___ fight? ___ They leave that ___ all to the poor! ___ Yeah!
Treat - ing peo - ple just like pawns in ___ chess, ___ Wait till their Judge-ment Day comes. ___ Yeah!

Interlude

D5 E5   F5 F#5 F5   E5   D5 E5   G5 F#5

Gtrs. 1 & 2

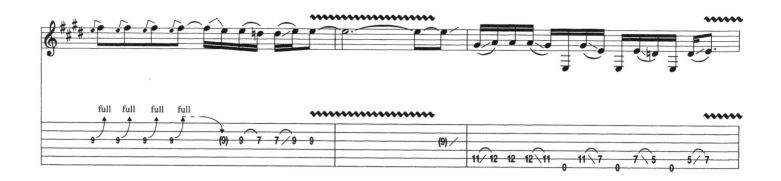

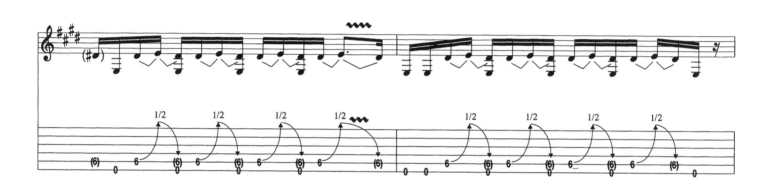

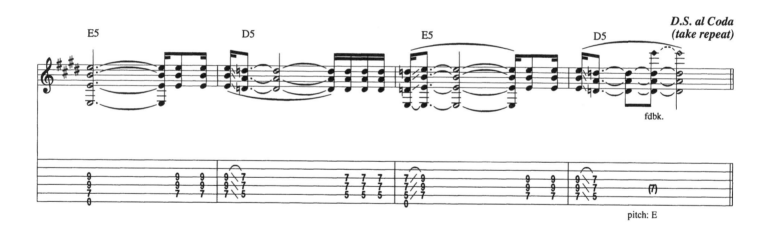

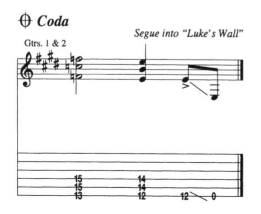

Segue into "Luke's Wall"

Luke's Wall

Words and Music by Frank Iommi, John Osbourne, William Ward and Terence Butler

*Tape speeds up; last chord sounds 10 1/2 steps higher.

Paranoid

Words and Music by Anthony Iommi, John Osbourne, William Ward and Terence Butler

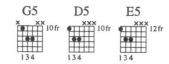

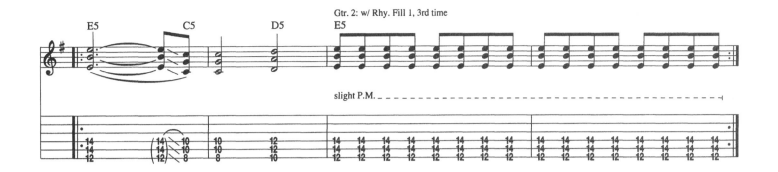

Verse

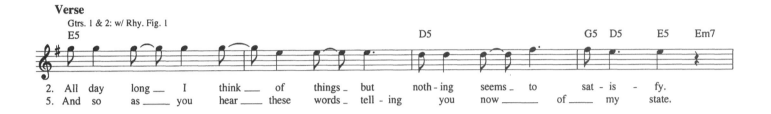

2. All day long __ I think __ of things __ but noth-ing seems __ to sat-is- fy.
5. And so as ___ you hear ___ these words __ tell-ing you now ___ of ___ my state.

To Coda ⊕

Think I'll lose __ my mind __ if I ___ don't find __ some-thing __ to pass it by.
I tell you __ to en - joy life, __ I wish __ I could __ but it's too late.

Bridge

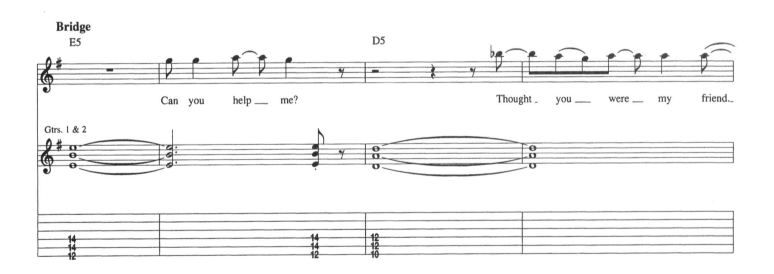

Can you help __ me?   Thought __ you __ were __ my friend. __

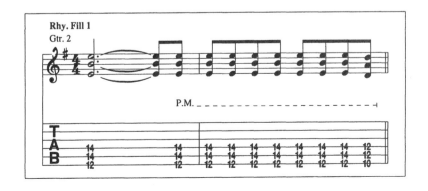

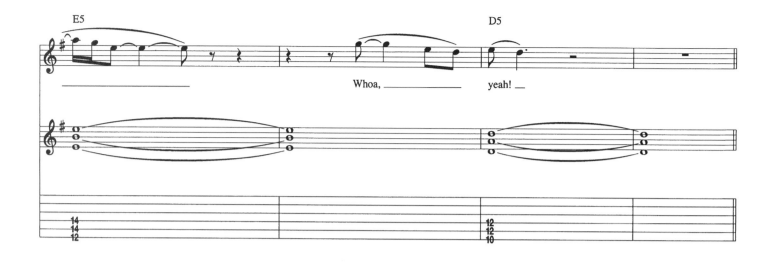

Interlude

slight P.M.

Verse

Gtrs. 1 & 2: w/ Rhy. Fig. 1

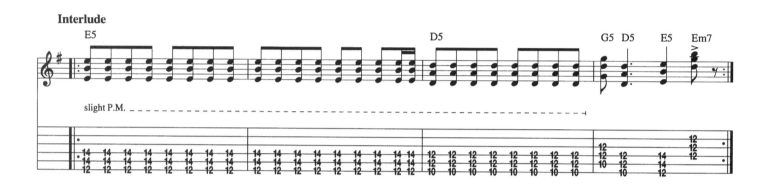

3. I need some-one to ___ show me ___ the things ___ in life ___ that I can't find.

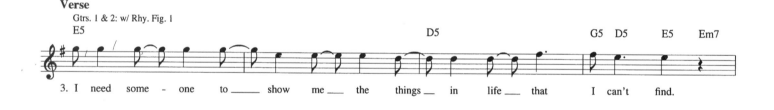

I can't see ___ the things ___ that make ___ true hap - pi - ness, ___ I must be blind.

Guitar Solo

Gtr. 2: w/ Rhy. Fig. 1, 1st 4 meas., 4 times

*Gtr. 1

1 1/2

*With heavily distorted ring modulation effect in right channel.

18

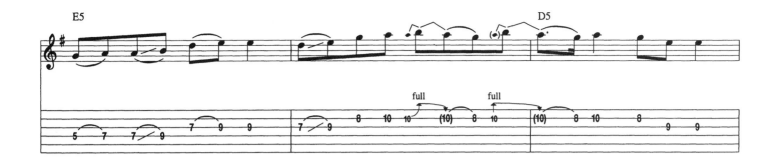

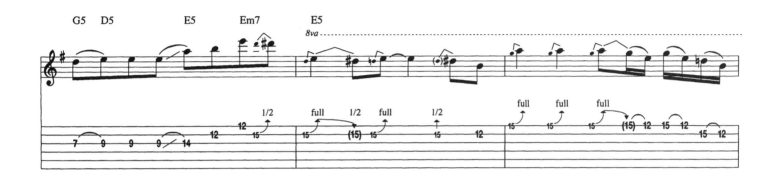

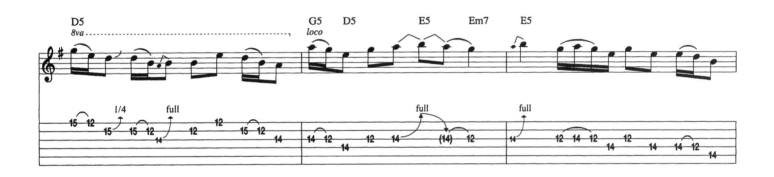

Interlude

D.S. al Coda

Gtrs. 1 & 2: w/ Rhy. Fig. 1,
1st 4 meas., 2 times

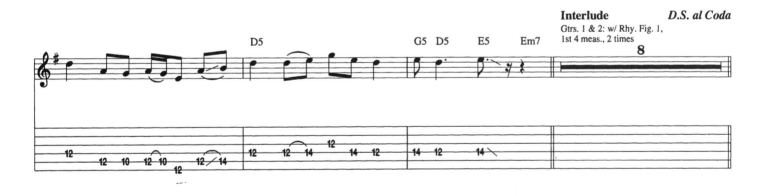

⊕ *Coda*

Outro

Gtrs. 1 & 2: w/ Rhy. Fig. 1, 1st 7 meas.

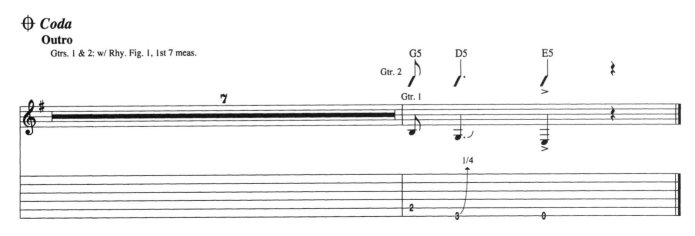

Planet Caravan

Words and Music by Frank Iommi, John Osbourne, William Ward and Terence Butler

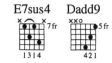

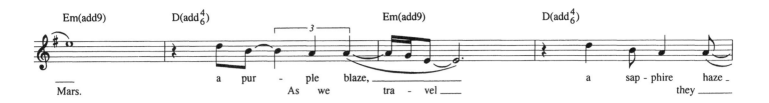

Mars.
a pur - ple blaze, _____ a sap - phire haze _____
As we tra - vel _____ they _____

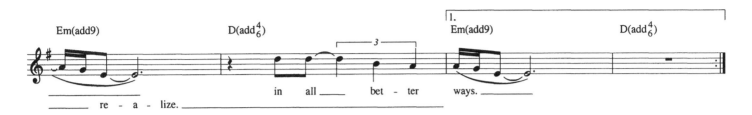

1.

_____ re - a - lize.
in all _____ bet - ter ways. _____

2.

Guitar Solo

Gtr. 1

*Em(add9)   D(add⁴₆)   Em(add9)

*Chord symbols implied by bass.

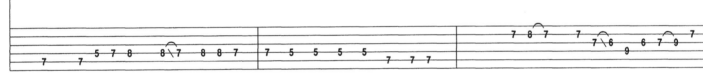

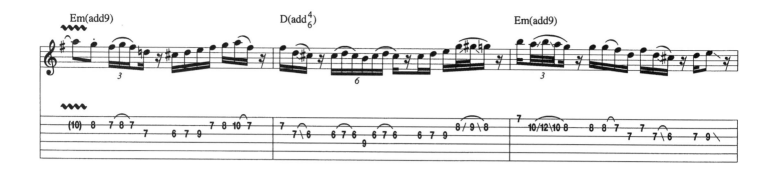

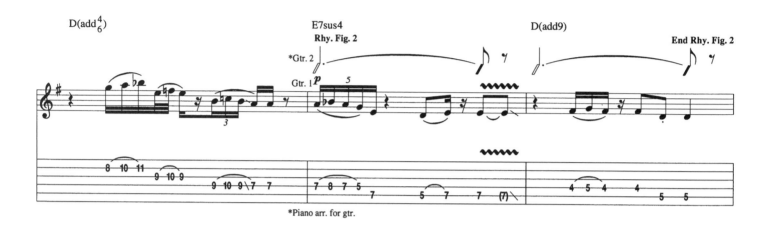

*Piano arr. for gtr.

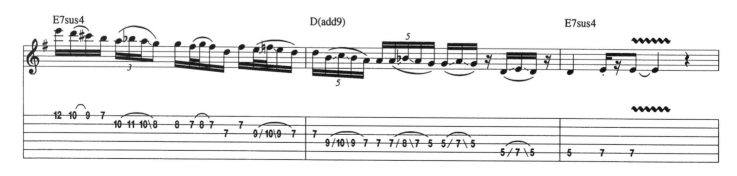

Iron Man

Words and Music by Frank Iommi, John Osbourne, William Ward and Terence Butler

Intro
Slow Rock ♩ = 69

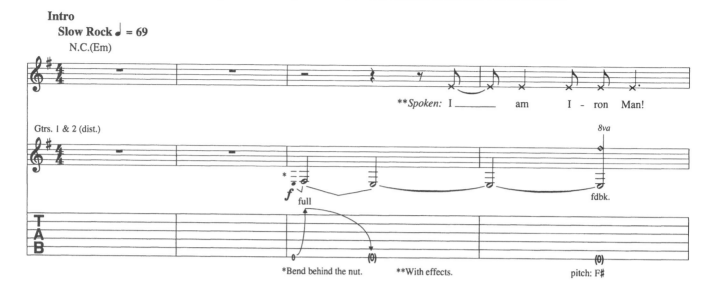

*Bend behind the nut.   **With effects.   pitch: F#

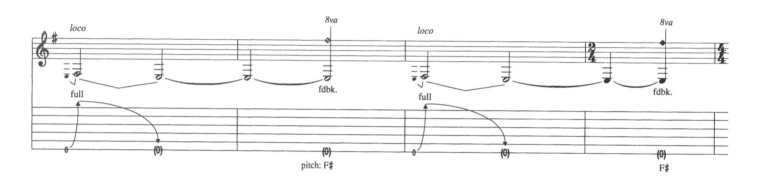

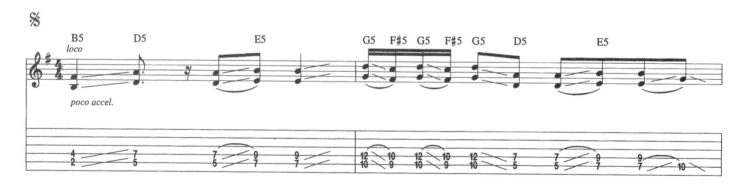

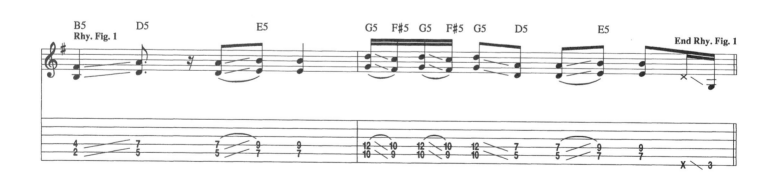

Guitar Solo

Gtr. 2 tacet

Gtr. 1   N.C.(C#m)

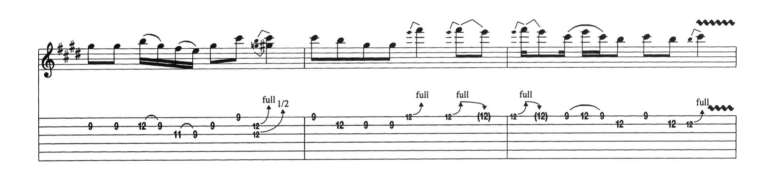

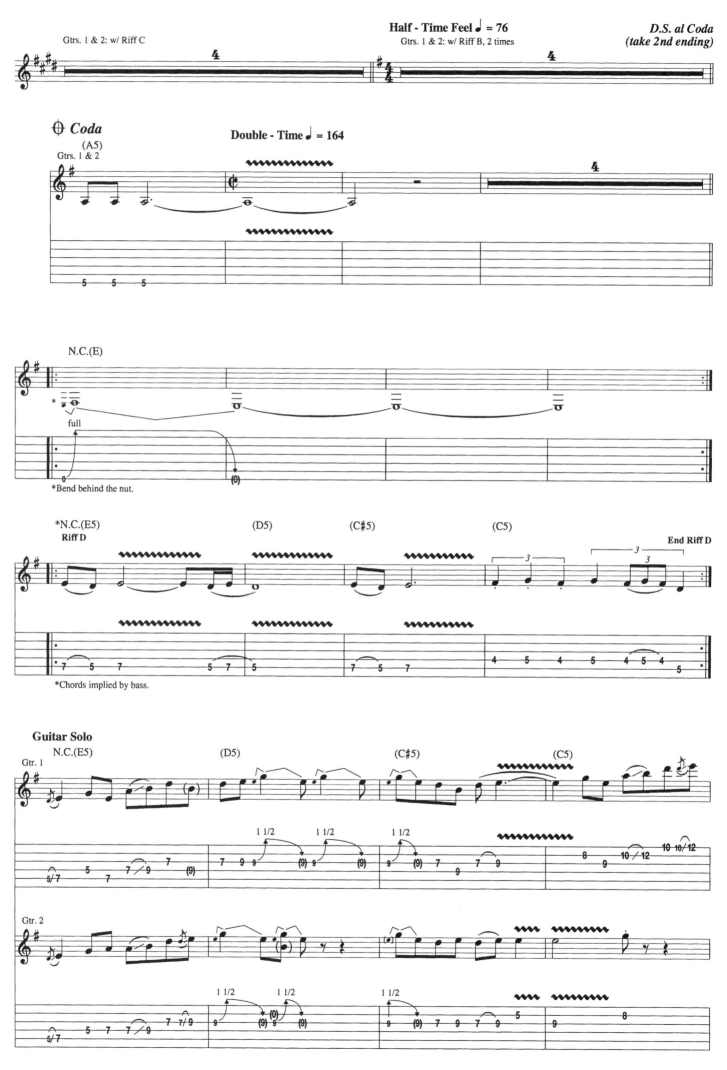

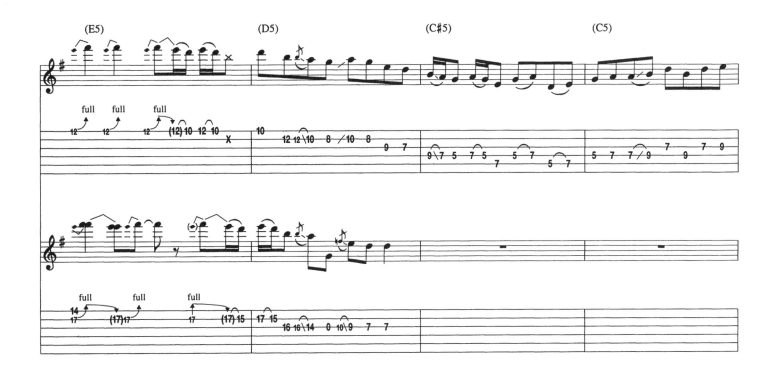

Outro

Gtrs. 1 & 2: w/ Riff D, 3 times

N.C.(E5)

Gtrs. 1 & 2

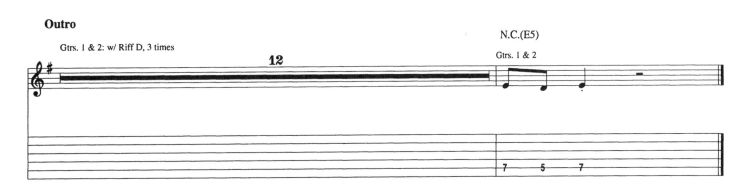

Electric Funeral

Words and Music by Frank Iommi, John Osbourne, William Ward and Terence Butler

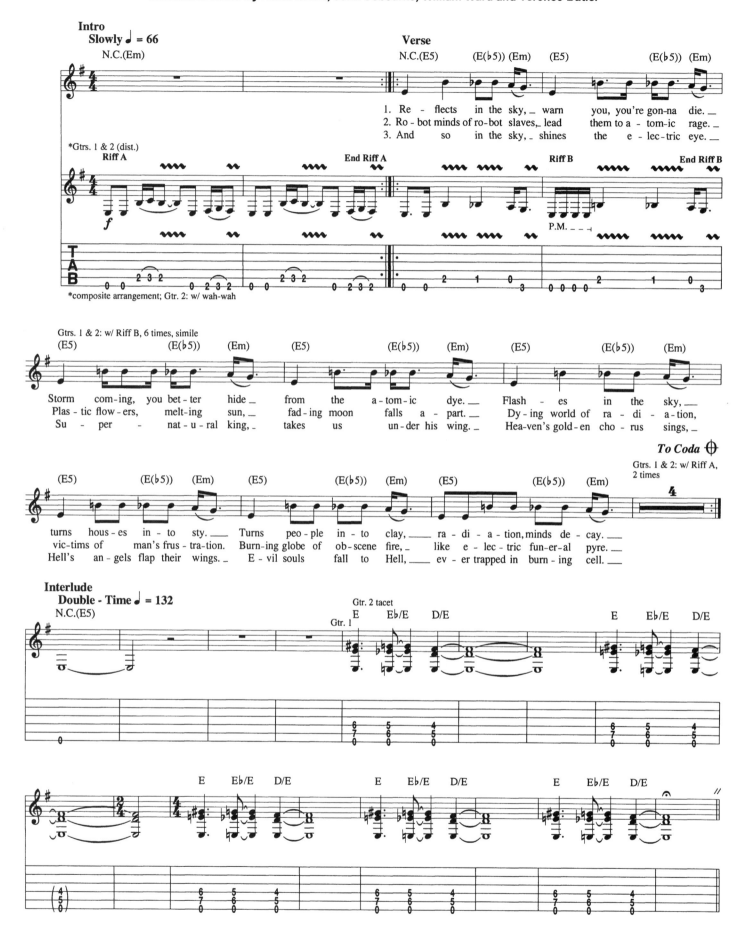

is the __ burn - ing flame. __ 'Lec - tric __ fun - 'ral. __ 'Lec - tric __ fun - 'ral.

'Lec - tric __ fun - 'ral. E - lec - tric __ fun - 'ral.

D.C. al Coda
Slower ♩ = 66

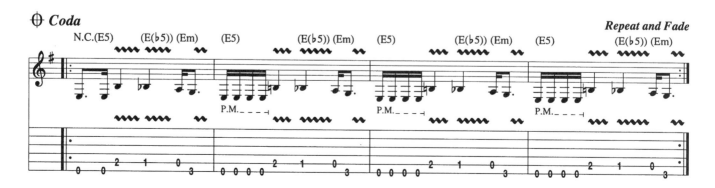

⊕ *Coda*

Repeat and Fade

Hand of Doom

Words and Music by Frank Iommi, John Osbourne, William Ward and Terence Butler

*Distortion pedal produces fdbk.

Additional Lyrics

3. Now you know the scene.
   Your skin starts turning green.
   Your eyes no longer see,
   Life's Reality.
   Push the needle in,
   Face that sickly grin.
   Holes are in your skin,
   Caused by deadly pin.

4. Head starts spinning 'round,
   Fall down to the ground.
   Feel your body heave,
   Death hand starts to weave.
   It's too late to turn,
   You don't want to learn.
   Price of life you hide.
   Now you're gonna die.

Rat Salad

Words and Music by Frank Iommi, John Osbourne, William Ward and Terence Butler

*composite arrangement
**vol. swell

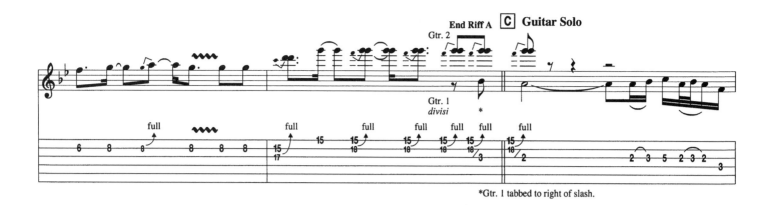

*Gtr. 1 tabbed to right of slash.

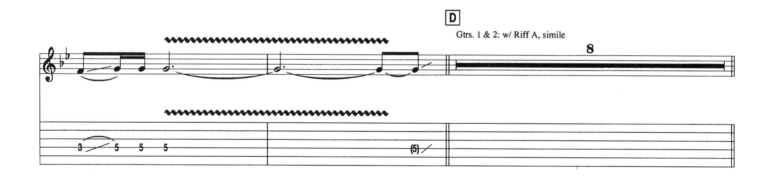

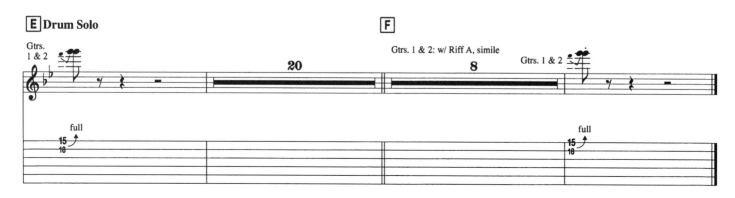

Jack the Stripper

Words and Music by Frank Iommi, John Osbourne, William Ward and Terence Butler

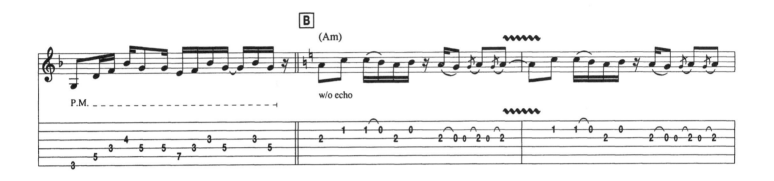

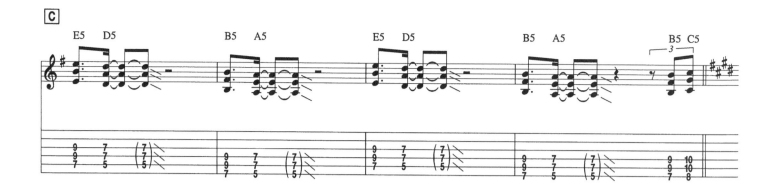

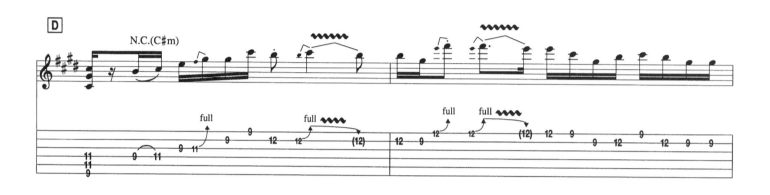

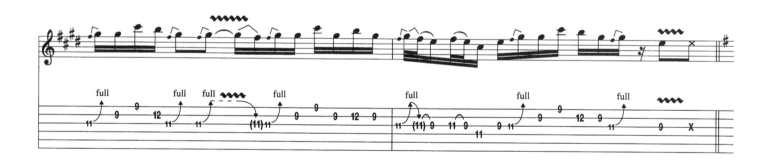

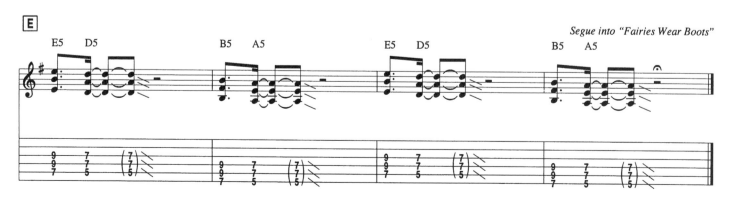

Segue into "Fairies Wear Boots"

Fairies Wear Boots

Words and Music by Frank Iommi, John Osbourne, William Ward and Terence Butler

Guitar Notation Legend

Guitar Music can be notated three different ways: on a *musical staff*, in *tablature*, and in *rhythm slashes*.

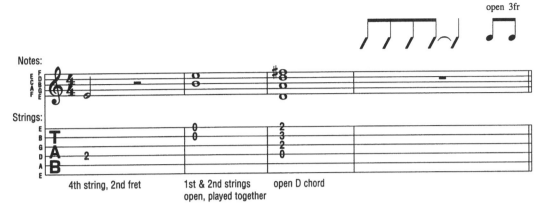

RHYTHM SLASHES are written above the staff. Strum chords in the rhythm indicated. Use the chord diagrams found at the top of the first page of the transcription for the appropriate chord voicings. Round noteheads indicate single notes.

THE MUSICAL STAFF shows pitches and rhythms and is divided by bar lines into measures. Pitches are named after the first seven letters of the alphabet.

TABLATURE graphically represents the guitar fingerboard. Each horizontal line represents a a string, and each number represents a fret.

4th string, 2nd fret

1st & 2nd strings open, played together

open D chord

Definitions for Special Guitar Notation

HALF-STEP BEND: Strike the note and bend up 1/2 step.

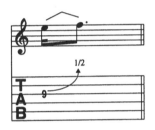

WHOLE-STEP BEND: Strike the note and bend up one step.

GRACE NOTE BEND: Strike the note and bend up as indicated. The first note does not take up any time.

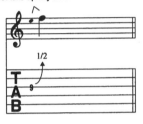

SLIGHT (MICROTONE) BEND: Strike the note and bend up 1/4 step.

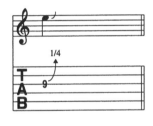

BEND AND RELEASE: Strike the note and bend up as indicated, then release back to the original note. Only the first note is struck.

PRE-BEND: Bend the note as indicated, then strike it.

PRE-BEND AND RELEASE: Bend the note as indicated. Strike it and release the bend back to the original note.

UNISON BEND: Strike the two notes simultaneously and bend the lower note up to the pitch of the higher.

VIBRATO: The string is vibrated by rapidly bending and releasing the note with the fretting hand.

WIDE VIBRATO: The pitch is varied to a greater degree by vibrating with the fretting hand.

HAMMER-ON: Strike the first (lower) note with one finger, then sound the higher note (on the same string) with another finger by fretting it without picking.

PULL-OFF: Place both fingers on the notes to be sounded. Strike the first note and without picking, pull the finger off to sound the second (lower) note.

LEGATO SLIDE: Strike the first note and then slide the same fret-hand finger up or down to the second note. The second note is not struck.

SHIFT SLIDE: Same as legato slide, except the second note is struck.

TRILL: Very rapidly alternate between the notes indicated by continuously hammering on and pulling off.

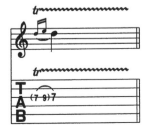

TAPPING: Hammer ("tap") the fret indicated with the pick-hand index or middle finger and pull off to the note fretted by the fret hand.

NATURAL HARMONIC: Strike the note while the fret-hand lightly touches the string directly over the fret indicated.

PINCH HARMONIC: The note is fretted normally and a harmonic is produced by adding the edge of the thumb or the tip of the index finger of the pick hand to the normal pick attack.

HARP HARMONIC: The note is fretted normally and a harmonic is produced by gently resting the pick hand's index finger directly above the indicated fret (in parentheses) while the pick hand's thumb or pick assists by plucking the appropriate string.

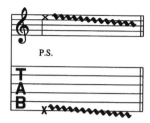

PICK SCRAPE: The edge of the pick is rubbed down (or up) the string, producing a scratchy sound.

MUFFLED STRINGS: A percussive sound is produced by laying the fret hand across the string(s) without depressing, and striking them with the pick hand.

PALM MUTING: The note is partially muted by the pick hand lightly touching the string(s) just before the bridge.

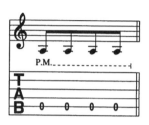

RAKE: Drag the pick across the strings indicated with a single motion.

TREMOLO PICKING: The note is picked as rapidly and continuously as possible.

ARPEGGIATE: Play the notes of the chord indicated by quickly rolling them from bottom to top.

VIBRATO BAR DIVE AND RETURN: The pitch of the note or chord is dropped a specified number of steps (in rhythm) then returned to the original pitch.

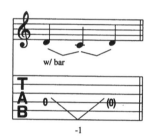

VIBRATO BAR SCOOP: Depress the bar just before striking the note, then quickly release the bar.

VIBRATO BAR DIP: Strike the note and then immediately drop a specified number of steps, then release back to the original pitch.

Additional Musical Definitions

(accent) • Accentuate note (play it louder)

(accent) • Accentuate note with great intensity

(staccato) • Play the note short

⊓ • Downstroke

∨ • Upstroke

D.S. al Coda • Go back to the sign (𝄋), then play until the measure marked "***To Coda***," then skip to the section labelled "***Coda***."

D.S. al Fine • Go back to the beginning of the song and play until the measure marked "***Fine***" (end).

Rhy. Fig. • Label used to recall a recurring accompaniment pattern (usually chordal).

Riff • Label used to recall composed, melodic lines (usually single notes) which recur.

Fill • Label used to identify a brief melodic figure which is to be inserted into the arrangement.

Rhy. Fill • A chordal version of a Fill.

tacet • Instrument is silent (drops out).

• Repeat measures between signs.

• When a repeated section has different endings, play the first ending only the first time and the second ending only the second time.

NOTE: Tablature numbers in parentheses mean:
1. The note is being sustained over a system (note in standard notation is tied), or
2. The note is sustained, but a new articulation (such as a hammer-on, pull-off, slide or vibrato begins, or
3. The note is a barely audible "ghost" note (note in standard notation is also in parentheses).

GUITAR *signature licks*

Signature Licks book/audio packs provide a step-by-step breakdown of "right from the record" riffs, licks, and solos so you can jam along with your favorite bands. They contain performance notes and an overview of each artist's or group's style, with note-for-note transcriptions in notes and tab. The online audio tracks feature full-band demos at both normal and slow speeds.

AC/DC
14041352......................$24.99

AEROSMITH 1973-1979
00695106......................$24.99

AEROSMITH 1979-1998
00695219......................$22.95

DUANE ALLMAN
00696042......................$24.99

BEST OF CHET ATKINS
00695752......................$24.99

AVENGED SEVENFOLD
00696473......................$24.99

THE BEATLES
00298845......................$24.99

BEST OF THE BEATLES FOR ACOUSTIC GUITAR
00695453...................... $26.99

THE BEATLES HITS
00695049......................$24.95

JEFF BECK
00696427......................$24.99

BEST OF GEORGE BENSON
00695418......................$24.99

BEST OF BLACK SABBATH
00695249......................$24.99

BON JOVI
00696380...................... $22.99

ROY BUCHANAN
00696654...................... $22.99

KENNY BURRELL
00695830......................$27.99

BEST OF CHARLIE CHRISTIAN
00695584......................$24.99

BEST OF ERIC CLAPTON
00695038......................$24.99

ERIC CLAPTON – FROM THE ALBUM UNPLUGGED
00695250......................$24.99

THE DOORS
00695373......................$22.95

DEEP PURPLE – GREATEST HITS
00695625......................$24.99

DREAM THEATER
00111943......................$27.99

ESSENTIAL JAZZ GUITAR
00695875......................$19.99

FLEETWOOD MAC
00696416...................... $22.99

ROBBEN FORD
00695903...................... $22.95

BEST OF GRANT GREEN
00695747......................$24.99

PETER GREEN
00145386......................$24.99

BEST OF GUNS N' ROSES
00695183......................$24.99

THE BEST OF BUDDY GUY
00695186......................$22.99

JIM HALL
00695848 ....$29.99

JIMI HENDRIX
00696560......................$27.99

JIMI HENDRIX – VOLUME 2
00695835 ....$24.99

JOHN LEE HOOKER
00695894......................$24.99

BEST OF JAZZ GUITAR
00695586......................$29.99

ERIC JOHNSON
00699317......................$27.99

ROBERT JOHNSON
00695264......................$24.99

BARNEY KESSEL
00696009......................$24.99

THE ESSENTIAL ALBERT KING
00695713......................$24.99

B.B. KING – BLUES LEGEND
00696039......................$22.99

B.B. KING – THE DEFINITIVE COLLECTION
00695635......................$22.99

MARK KNOPFLER
00695178......................$24.99

LYNYRD SKYNYRD
00695872......................$24.99

THE BEST OF YNGWIE MALMSTEEN
00695669......................$24.99

BEST OF PAT MARTINO
00695632......................$24.99

MEGADETH
00696421 ....$22.99

WES MONTGOMERY
00695387......................$24.99

BEST OF NIRVANA
00695483......................$24.95

VERY BEST OF OZZY OSBOURNE
00695431...................... $22.99

BRAD PAISLEY
00696379......................$22.99

BEST OF JOE PASS
00695730......................$24.99

TOM PETTY
00696021......................$24.99

PINK FLOYD
00103659......................$27.99

THE GUITARS OF ELVIS
00174800......................$22.99

BEST OF QUEEN
00695097......................$24.99

RADIOHEAD
00109304......................$24.99

BEST OF RAGE AGAINST THE MACHINE
00695480......................$24.99

JERRY REED
00118236 ....$22.99

BEST OF DJANGO REINHARDT
00695660......................$27.99

BEST OF ROCK 'N' ROLL GUITAR
00695559......................$24.99

BEST OF ROCKABILLY GUITAR
00695785......................$22.99

BEST OF CARLOS SANTANA
00174664 ....$22.99

SLASH
00696576......................$22.99

SLAYER
00121281......................$22.99

BEST OF SOUTHERN ROCK
00695560......................$19.95

STEELY DAN
00696015......................$22.99

MIKE STERN
00695800......................$27.99

BEST OF SURF GUITAR
00695822......................$22.99

STEVE VAI
00673247......................$24.99

STEVE VAI – ALIEN LOVE SECRETS: THE NAKED VAMPS
00695223......................$27.99

STEVE VAI – FIRE GARDEN: THE NAKED VAMPS
00695166 ....$22.95

STEVE VAI – THE ULTRA ZONE: NAKED VAMPS
00695684......................$22.95

VAN HALEN
00110227......................$27.99

THE GUITAR STYLE OF STEVIE RAY VAUGHAN
00695155......................$24.95

BEST OF THE VENTURES
00695772......................$24.99

THE WHO – 2ND ED.
00695561 ....$22.95

JOHNNY WINTER
00695951......................$24.99

YES
00113120......................$24.99

BEST OF ZZ TOP
00695738......................$24.99

HAL•LEONARD®

www.halleonard.com

COMPLETE DESCRIPTIONS AND SONGLISTS ONLINE!

Prices, contents and availability subject to change without notice.

1222

305

RECORDED VERSIONS®
The Best Note-For-Note Transcriptions Available

AUTHENTIC TRANSCRIPTIONS WITH NOTES AND TABLATURE

00690603	Aerosmith – O Yeah! Ultimate Hits	$29.99
00690178	Alice in Chains – Acoustic	$22.99
00694865	Alice in Chains – Dirt	$19.99
00694925	Alice in Chains – Jar of Flies/Sap	$19.99
00691091	Alice Cooper – Best of	$24.99
00690958	Duane Allman – Guitar Anthology	$29.99
00694932	Allman Brothers Band – Volume 1	$29.99
00694933	Allman Brothers Band – Volume 2	$27.99
00694934	Allman Brothers Band – Volume 3	$29.99
00690945	Alter Bridge – Blackbird	$24.99
00123558	Arctic Monkeys – AM	$24.99
00214869	Avenged Sevenfold – Best of 2005-2013	$29.99
00690489	Beatles – 1	$24.99
00694929	Beatles – 1962-1966	$27.99
00694930	Beatles – 1967-1970	$29.99
00694880	Beatles – Abbey Road	$19.99
00694832	Beatles – Acoustic Guitar	$27.99
00690110	Beatles – White Album (Book 1)	$19.99
00692385	Chuck Berry	$24.99
00147787	Black Crowes – Best of	$24.99
00690149	Black Sabbath	$19.99
00690901	Black Sabbath – Best of	$22.99
00691010	Black Sabbath – Heaven and Hell	$24.99
00690148	Black Sabbath – Master of Reality	$19.99
00690142	Black Sabbath – Paranoid	$19.99
00148544	Michael Bloomfield – Guitar Anthology	$24.99
00158600	Joe Bonamassa – Blues of Desperation	$24.99
00198117	Joe Bonamassa – Muddy Wolf at Red Rocks	$24.99
00283540	Joe Bonamassa – Redemption	$24.99
00358863	Joe Bonamassa – Royal Tea	$24.99
00690913	Boston	$22.99
00690491	David Bowie – Best of	$22.99
00286503	Big Bill Broonzy – Guitar Collection	$19.99
00690261	The Carter Family Collection	$19.99
00691079	Johnny Cash – Best of	$24.99
00690936	Eric Clapton – Complete Clapton	$34.99
00694869	Eric Clapton – Unplugged	$24.99
00124873	Eric Clapton – Unplugged (Deluxe)	$29.99
00138731	Eric Clapton & Friends – The Breeze	$24.99
00139967	Coheed & Cambria – In Keeping Secrets of Silent Earth: 3	$24.99
00141704	Jesse Cook – Works, Vol. 1	$19.99
00288787	Creed – Greatest Hits	$22.99
00690819	Creedence Clearwater Revival	$27.99
00690648	Jim Croce – Very Best of	$19.99
00690572	Steve Cropper – Soul Man	$22.99
00690613	Crosby, Stills & Nash – Best of	$29.99
00690784	Def Leppard – Best of	$24.99
00694831	Derek and the Dominos – Layla & Other Assorted Love Songs	$24.99
00291164	Dream Theater – Distance Over Time	$24.99
00278631	Eagles – Greatest Hits 1971-1975	$22.99
00278632	Eagles – Very Best of	$39.99
00690515	Extreme II – Pornograffiti	$24.99
00150257	John Fahey – Guitar Anthology	$24.99
00690664	Fleetwood Mac – Best of	$24.99
00691024	Foo Fighters – Greatest Hits	$24.99
00120220	Robben Ford – Guitar Anthology	$29.99
00295410	Rory Gallagher – Blues	$24.99
00139460	Grateful Dead – Guitar Anthology	$34.99
00691190	Peter Green – Best of	$24.99

00287517	Greta Van Fleet – Anthem of the Peaceful Army	$22.99
00287515	Greta Van Fleet – From the Fires	$19.99
00694798	George Harrison – Anthology	$24.99
00692930	Jimi Hendrix – Are You Experienced?	$29.99
00692931	Jimi Hendrix – Axis: Bold As Love	$24.99
00690304	Jimi Hendrix – Band of Gypsys	$27.99
00694944	Jimi Hendrix – Blues	$29.99
00692932	Jimi Hendrix – Electric Ladyland	$27.99
00660029	Buddy Holly – Best of	$24.99
00200446	Iron Maiden – Guitar Tab	$34.99
00694912	Eric Johnson – Ah Via Musicom	$24.99
00690271	Robert Johnson – Transcriptions	$27.99
00690427	Judas Priest – Best of	$24.99
00690492	B.B. King – Anthology	$29.99
00130447	B.B. King – Live at the Regal	$19.99
00690134	Freddie King – Collection	$22.99
00327968	Marcus King – El Dorado	$22.99
00690157	Kiss – Alive	$19.99
00690356	Kiss – Alive II	$24.99
00291163	Kiss – Very Best of	$24.99
00345767	Greg Koch – Best of	$29.99
00690377	Kris Kristofferson – Guitar Collection	$22.99
00690834	Lamb of God – Ashes of the Wake	$24.99
00690525	George Lynch – Best of	$29.99
00690955	Lynyrd Skynyrd – All-Time Greatest Hits	$24.99
00694954	Lynyrd Skynyrd – New Best of	$24.99
00690577	Yngwie Malmsteen – Anthology	$29.99
00694896	John Mayall with Eric Clapton – Blues Breakers	$19.99
00694952	Megadeth – Countdown to Extinction	$24.99
00276065	Megadeth – Greatest Hits: Back to the Start	$27.99
00694951	Megadeth – Rust in Peace	$27.99
00690011	Megadeth – Youthanasia	$24.99
00209876	Metallica – Hardwired to Self-Destruct	$24.99
00690646	Pat Metheny – One Quiet Night	$24.99
00102591	Wes Montgomery – Guitar Anthology	$27.99
00691092	Gary Moore – Best of	$27.99
00694802	Gary Moore – Still Got the Blues	$24.99
00355456	Alanis Morisette – Jagged Little Pill	$22.99
00690611	Nirvana	$24.99
00694913	Nirvana – In Utero	$22.99
00694883	Nirvana – Nevermind	$19.99
00690026	Nirvana – Unplugged in New York	$19.99
00265439	Nothing More – Tab Collection	$24.99
00243349	Opeth – Best of	$22.99
00690499	Tom Petty – Definitive Guitar Collection	$24.99
00121933	Pink Floyd – Acoustic Guitar Collection	$27.99
00690428	Pink Floyd – Dark Side of the Moon	$22.99
00244637	Pink Floyd – Guitar Anthology	$24.99
00239799	Pink Floyd – The Wall	$27.99
00690789	Poison – Best of	$22.99
00690925	Prince – Very Best of	$24.99
00690003	Queen – Classic Queen	$24.99
00694975	Queen – Greatest Hits	$25.99
00694910	Rage Against the Machine	$24.99
00119834	Rage Against the Machine – Guitar Anthology	$24.99
00690426	Ratt – Best of	$24.99
00690055	Red Hot Chili Peppers – Blood Sugar Sex Magik	$19.99

00690379	Red Hot Chili Peppers – Californication	$22.99
00690673	Red Hot Chili Peppers – Greatest Hits	$24.99
00690852	Red Hot Chili Peppers – Stadium Arcadium	$29.99
00690511	Django Reinhardt – Definitive Collection	$24.99
00690014	Rolling Stones – Exile on Main Street	$24.99
00690631	Rolling Stones – Guitar Anthology	$34.99
00323854	Rush – The Spirit of Radio: Greatest Hits, 1974-1987	$22.99
00173534	Santana – Guitar Anthology	$29.99
00276350	Joe Satriani – What Happens Next	$24.99
00690566	Scorpions – Best of	$24.99
00690604	Bob Seger – Guitar Collection	$24.99
00234543	Ed Sheeran – Divide*	$19.99
00691114	Slash – Guitar Anthology	$34.99
00690813	Slayer – Guitar Collection	$24.99
00690419	Slipknot	$22.99
00316982	Smashing Pumpkins – Greatest Hits	$24.99
00690912	Soundgarden – Guitar Anthology	$24.99
00120004	Steely Dan – Best of	$27.99
00322564	Stone Temple Pilots – Thank You	$22.99
00690520	Styx – Guitar Collection	$22.99
00120081	Sublime	$22.99
00690531	System of a Down – Toxicity	$19.99
00694824	James Taylor – Best of	$19.99
00694887	Thin Lizzy – Best of	$22.99
00253237	Trivium – Guitar Tab Anthology	$24.99
00690683	Robin Trower – Bridge of Sighs	$19.99
00156024	Steve Vai – Guitar Anthology	$39.99
00660137	Steve Vai – Passion & Warfare	$29.99
00295076	Van Halen – 30 Classics	$29.99
00690024	Stevie Ray Vaughan – Couldn't Stand the Weather	$22.99
00660058	Stevie Ray Vaughan – Lightnin' Blues 1983-1987	$29.99
00217455	Stevie Ray Vaughan – Plays Slow Blues	$24.99
00694835	Stevie Ray Vaughan – The Sky Is Crying	$24.99
00690015	Stevie Ray Vaughan – Texas Flood	$22.99
00694789	Muddy Waters – Deep Blues	$27.99
00152161	Doc Watson – Guitar Anthology	$24.99
00690071	Weezer (The Blue Album)	$22.99
00237811	White Stripes – Greatest Hits	$24.99
00117511	Whitesnake – Guitar Collection	$24.99
00122303	Yes – Guitar Collection	$24.99
00690443	Frank Zappa – Hot Rats	$22.99
00121684	ZZ Top – Early Classics	$27.99
00690589	ZZ Top – Guitar Anthology	$24.99

COMPLETE SERIES LIST ONLINE!

www.halleonard.com

Prices and availability subject to change without notice.
*Tab transcriptions only.

0622

272